curiou?about

ATLANTIS

BY GILLIA M. OLSON

AMICUS LEARNING

What are you

curious about?

Curious About is published by
Amicus Learning, an imprint of Amicus
P.O. Box 227
Mankato, MN 56002
www.amicuspublishing.us

Editor: Ana Brauer
Series Designer: Kathleen Petelinsek
Book Designer and Photo Researcher: Emily Dietz

Library of Congress Cataloging-in-Publication Data
Names: Olson, Gillia M., author.
Title: Curious about Atlantis / by Gillia M. Olson.
Description: Mankato, MN : Amicus Learning, [2025] | Series: Curious about unexplained mysteries | Includes bibliographical references and index. | Audience: Ages 6–9 years | Audience: Grades 2–3 | Summary: "Does the lost city of Atlantis really exist? Learn about this unexplained mystery in this question-and-answer book for elementary-aged readers. Includes infographics, table of contents, glossary, books and websites for further research, and index"—Provided by publisher.
Identifiers: LCCN 2024016032 (print) | LCCN 2024016033 (ebook) | ISBN 9798892000925 (lib. bdg.) | ISBN 9798892001502 (paperback) | ISBN 9798892002080 (ebook)
Subjects: LCSH: Atlantis (Legendary place)—Juvenile literature.
Classification: LCC GN751 .O57 2025 (print) | LCC GN751 (ebook) | DDC 398.23/4—dc23/eng/20240527
LC record available at https://lccn.loc.gov/2024016032
LC ebook record available at https://lccn.loc.gov/2024016033

Photos Credits: Alamy/Chronicle, 15, TCD - Prod.DB, 21; Dreamstime/Valerijs Jegorovs, 6–7, Yutthaphong Wiangsimma, 2, 11; FreePik/studioworkstock, 2, 5; Getty Images/Pictures from History, 19; Noun Project/MihiMihi, 22, 23, Muhammad Atiq, 22, 23; Pixabay/Hansuan_Fabregas, cover, 1; Public Domain/unknown, 3, 16–17; Science Source/Mikkel Juul Jensen, 8–9; Shutterstock/Fer Gregory, 20, Sergey Ksen, 14, Stefanos Kyriazis, 4, Vikks, 12–13

Printed in China

CHAPTER ONE

Is Atlantis real?

According to legend, Atlantis was a great **ancient** city. It no longer exists. No one knows for sure if it ever did. An ancient Greek named Plato wrote about it in 360 **BC**. That was about 2,400 years ago. His writing is all we know about it.

DID YOU KNOW?
Plato said Atlantis existed 9,000 years before he wrote about it.

Many people picture the lost city of Atlantis as an underwater palace.

Where was it?

People have a lot of ideas, but no one really knows where Atlantis was.

Plato wrote that Atlantis was a huge island past the Pillars of Hercules. No one knows for sure where Plato meant. Today, the Pillars of Hercules are two points of land. They are on either side of a waterway near Spain.

What did Atlantis look like?

Atlantis was surrounded by rings of water.

Atlantis had circles of land inside one another. There was water in between each circle. People used bridges to cross the water. There was a great **temple** in the center island. The land grew many crops.

CHAPTER TWO

Who built Atlantis?

Plato said that Poseidon, the Greek god of the sea, created Atlantis. Poseidon's son, Atlas, was its first king. The people had what they needed to have good lives. They were humble. They followed the laws.

DID YOU KNOW?
In Plato's time, people worshipped many gods and goddesses.

Poseidon was one of the most powerful Greek gods.

What happened to Atlantis?

A huge wave could have caused Atlantis to sink beneath the water.

The story says that the Atlanteans became too full of pride. They became greedy. They no longer followed the laws. The gods wanted to punish them. The gods sent earthquakes and floods. Atlantis was destroyed in one day. It sank into the ocean.

What made the legend popular again?

A quartz crystal could have been used to power Atlantis. The crystals are said to make energy stronger.

In the 1800s, people who said they were **psychic** became interested in Atlantis. They said that Atlantis had advanced technology. Edgar Cayce claimed it used powerful crystals to power the city.

Edgar Cayce's ideas about Atlantis brought the myth back into popular culture.

DID YOU KNOW?

Today, more than half of Americans believe advanced civilizations, such as Atlantis, existed.

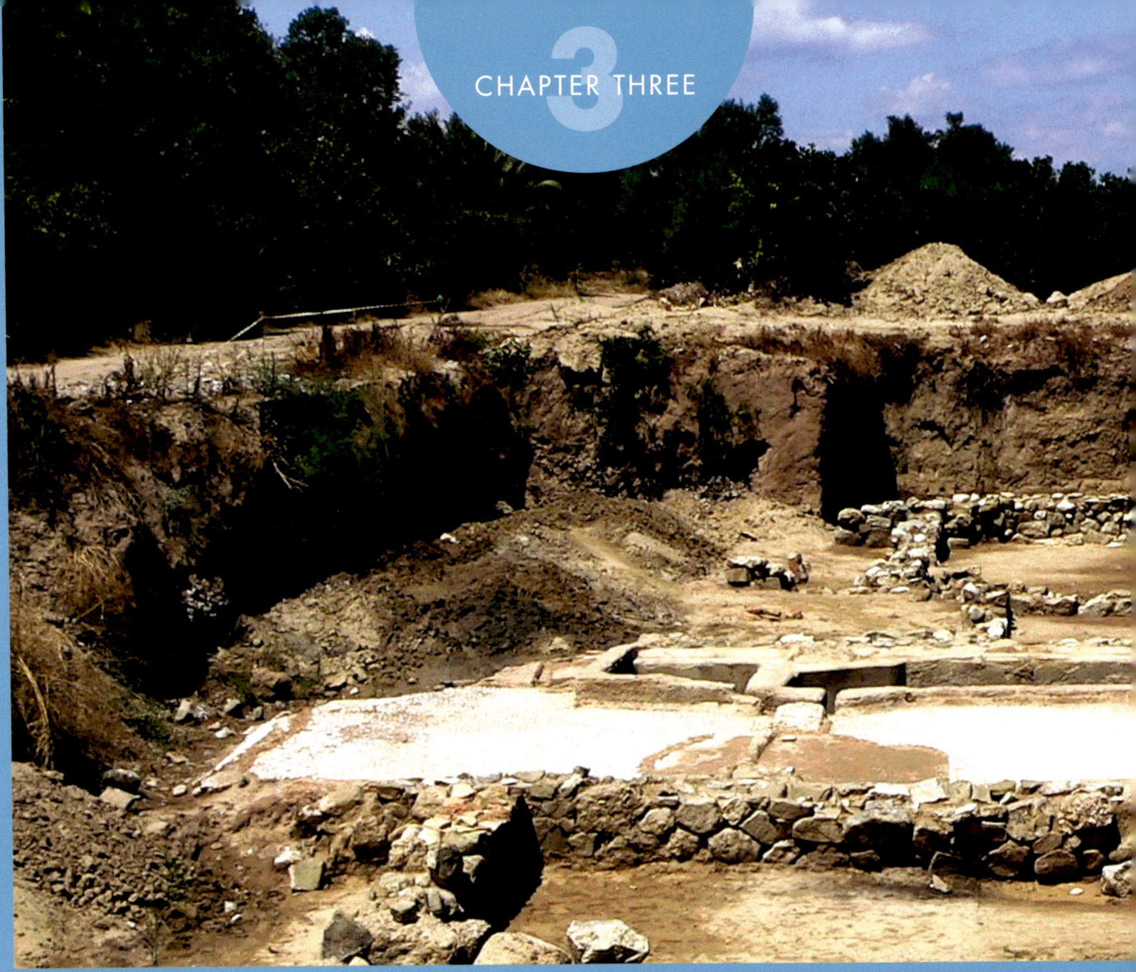

CHAPTER THREE

Why do people believe the myth?

In 2001, the ruins of Helike were found underground in Greece.

Earthquakes and floods have destroyed cities. One of these cities may have given Plato the idea for Atlantis. Helike (HEH-lee-kee) was a city near where Plato lived. The city fell into the sea during an earthquake. It happened only 10 years before Plato wrote about Atlantis.

What else could it be?

Most people think Plato's writings are just a story. Plato wanted to write about the best way for people to live. In his writings, Atlantis was a great **society**. But people's poor choices lead to the city's fall. The story of Atlantis might have been a warning about what not to do.

Plato (left) taught his beliefs to students in Greece.

What do people think now?

If Atlantis existed, it may be in ruins at the bottom of the Atlantic Ocean.

Many modern movies and books tell the legend of Atlantis. These stories show humans living in palaces under water. In real life, people continue to look for lost cities. No one has come up with **proof** of Atlantis yet. People will stay curious about the great city that sank into the sea.

DID YOU KNOW?
The superhero Aquaman is from Atlantis.

ASK MORE QUESTIONS

How do people search for lost cities in the water?

What happens during earthquakes?

Try a BIG QUESTION:
If Atlantis was really a city that was fully underwater, how would people live there?

SEARCH FOR ANSWERS

Search the library catalog or the Internet.
A librarian, teacher, or parent can help you.

Using Keywords
Find the looking glass.

Keywords are the most important words in your question.

?

If you want to know about:

- other lost cities, type: ANCIENT LOST CITIES
- earthquakes, type: EARTHQUAKE CAUSES AND EFFECTS

LEARN MORE

FIND GOOD SOURCES

Here are some good, safe sources you can use in your research.
Your librarian can help you find more.

Books

Atlantis by Meg Gaertner, 2022

What Do We Know About Atlantis?
by Emma Carlson Berne, 2022.

Internet Sites

TED-Ed: Real Life Sunken Cities
https://ed.ted.com/lessons/real-life-sunken-cities-peter-campbell
TED-Ed is a non-profit educational site with videos on many topics.

Wonderopolis: Where Is the Lost City of Atlantis?
https://wonderopolis.org/wonder/Where-Is-the-Lost-City-of-Atlantis
Wonderopolis is a non-profit site for students and their families.

Every effort has been made to ensure that these websites are appropriate for children. However, because of the nature of the Internet, it is impossible to guarantee that these sites will remain active indefinitely or that their contents will not be altered.

SHARE AND TAKE ACTION

Visit your local historical society.
Are there areas in your town where floods have happened? What damage did that do to the area?

Do you believe that Atlantis is real?
Research more before you come to a decision. Then, write a paragraph supporting your opinion. Share your writing with a family member.

Draw what you think Atlantis might look like.
Share your drawing with a friend.

GLOSSARY

ancient Very old; existing for many years.

BC Before Christ; the time before Jesus was born.

proof Facts or evidence that show something is true.

psychic A person who is sensitive to nonphysical forces.

society People who live together in organized communities with shared laws, traditions, and values.

temple A place of worship.

INDEX

About the Author

Gillia Olson is a skeptic by nature but loves all things paranormal. She stays curious and open-minded and hopes you will, too. She lives in southern Minnesota.